Living
Peacefully
with
CHRONIC
PAIN

Elizabeth Ann Johnston

Introduction

Learning to live with chronic pain is without a doubt the most difficult task God has given me thus far. I have had chronic pain for eighteen years. Most of those years, I have struggled with it, fought against it, waged my own little personal war with it, been angry with God over it, been angry with myself about it (I've done that best!), been angry with several doctors over it, gotten extremely depressed because of it, have thrown numerous temper tantrums, and, in general, have been just plain mad about it!

Looking back on it now, I feel that I must spend the rest of my life making amends to my family and the few remaining friends I have. Perhaps God is now calling me to write about being at peace with pain and to counsel others who are in similar circumstances is part of my penance for being such a pill about all of this for eighteen years. Thank God I am surrounded by forgiving people. They have forgiven me for my rude, crude, and socially unacceptable behavior, most of which I blame on heavy medications, but I fully understand that regardless of the medications, I must be responsible for my actions.

The good news is that I have learned from my experiences with chronic pain. I have learned that even though there may be times that I wish I were dead, pain will not kill me. Severe back and leg pain from four failed spinal surgeries did indeed create in me a stronger person. I have learned to exercise regardless of the arthritis pain in both knees. I have learned to use the power of my mind to keep me going when I have a major fibromyalgia flare up. I have learned to take better care of and to love my body as it is the only one I have! I have learned to gain strength from God and to be at peace with Him.

What a curse chronic pain was for me. And now, what a blessing it has become. I am a better person for having these experiences, and I thank God for them and for the continuing choice of living peacefully every day.

Thank You, God!

"If you love me you will keep my commandments. And I will ask the Father, and he will give you another advocate to be with you forever. This is the spirit of truth, whom the world cannot receive because it neither sees him nor knows him. You will know Him because He abides with you and He will be in you. ...

"I have said these things to you while I am still with you, but He the Advocate, the Holy Spirit, who the father will send in my name will teach you everything and remind you of all that I have said to you." (John 14:15, 25).

Jesus

Author's Note

When I was twelve years old, I was baptized in a Southern Baptist church surrounded by people whom I loved and completely respected. Many Christians would say that was when I received the Holy Spirit. This is what is true for me. If you are a follower of the teachings of Jesus Christ, you also believe in the Holy Trinity of Father, Son, and Holy Spirit.

If you have ever spent much time in prayer and meditation, you will most likely also believe in the power of the Holy Spirit. You may have a close relationship with God's mighty Advocate. What a powerful, wonderful, loving relationship it can be! At least, this is what I have discovered.

I believe that sometimes we spend too much time in prayer begging God for what we want — and, yes, even sometimes telling God what to do and how to do it. Can you imagine the nerve? We forget the absolute importance of shutting up and listening. It is when we get quiet that we hear the words or feel little nudges of the Holy Spirit, our Advocate, the One whom God our Father sent to us, to comfort us and guide us to do the right thing; it is there in that still small voice that God speaks to us. *God, we get so busy begging and complaining and trying to run our own agendas that we forget to say: Not my will, Father, but Yours. May Your will be done on earth as it is in heaven.*

It serves me well to quiet my mind and invite the Holy Spirit to guide me. It gives me great joy and amazing peace to tell you that I have written this little book, this small but ever-so-meaningful guide, as a conversation with my Advocate—whom I personally and ever-so-respectfully call "The Big Guy"—my friend, my confidante. My friends and family often hear me refer to Him simply as "HS." He has been with me at least since the age of twelve and has watched over me my entire life. He has helped me through some very difficult times, and our relationship is truly unique and special.

Therefore, it does not surprise me to be writing this as a conversation with the Holy Spirit. I certainly did not intend to do this. Yet here it is. Writing this conversation was as natural to me as talking to any other member of my family or to a close and dear friend.

My wish for you is that you may have your own unique and loving relationship with the mighty Holy Spirit. For herein lies the peace of God.

My Experience

It's Thursday, 5:34 p.m. I wanted to go to the fibromyalgia support group meeting tonight with my friend Patti, but I am not going because I am having severe spasms in my legs and sitting for any length of time at all makes the spasms worse. So I'm upset; actually, just plain ticked off, in addition to being in considerable pain.

With whom are you angry?

God! God! And only God, because He is not answering my prayers!

When you have done all that you can, we'll talk. Please remember that God did not leave you powerless; quite the contrary, for with God

I

you are amazingly powerful. When Jesus said, "With God, all things are possible," He meant it.

You must ask yourself this question: "What does healing look like for me through the eyes of God?"

So maybe this is the best it gets for me? Stuck in my house most of the time, popping pills to ease my pain and relax the muscle spasms so my life can be reasonably tolerable? Are you kidding me? Please say that You are kidding me, that this is some kind of a twisted joke, because I'm too young to live like this, to have so much pain all the time and be so limited in my activities! Please, dear God, say it isn't so!

Do you realize how wonderful your life is?

Wonderful? It doesn't feel very wonderful right now!

Perhaps your perception is clouded by your anger.

Perhaps; or maybe, just maybe, I'm sick and tired of feeling tired and in pain all of the time.

Do you honestly need me to bring to your attention what a wonderful life you have? You play Jimmy Stewart, and I'll be Clarence, the angel.

Very funny! Sometimes I feel like my life is a movie and we are all just playing particular roles. There are the major players: my husband, children and grandchildren, parents, close friends, and me. Then there are all of the extras, scene changes, and such. Often, I wonder who in the heck is directing.

Ah! Herein lays the source of your anger!

What?

You're not sure who's in charge. It's your life, but you have allowed your body to be in charge. You have given your power away. It feels odd because it's backwards.

It certainly feels backwards! But having fibromyalgia and chronic back and leg pain due to four spinal surgeries is a bit like having kids: the one who yells the loudest or acts out the most is the one who will get your attention. Sometimes I feel as though I'm just stamping out a small closet fire while my house is burning down around me.

I can understand your frustration. Let's take things one step at a time to help us get a proper perspective.

Sounds good to me. Where do we begin?

How about beginning with where you are now which under the present circumstances, is very much in your body? Remember I mentioned a bit earlier that you have been allowing your body to be in charge of your pain and your life. We want to get to a point where you are listening mostly to your heart. Your heart—God, Christ—will never, ever lead you astray. Chronic pain and fatigue tends to bring people down, and they forget to turn their lives over to God every day (or however often they need to turn it over throughout the day). But turning the negativity, the frustration, the fear—everything that is not love—over to God is crucial to living in that peaceful place.

I know what You are saying. Sometimes it seems as though I'm constantly giving all of my negative "stuff" over to God; then I take it back and begin to worry or feel frustrated or even bored. Then I say, "Oh, yeah, here, God, please take this from me." And of course He does—until five minutes later when I take it back again. It's a cycle.

Yes, but that's a great beginning. One day you have a good day, and you realize that God handled everything for you today. You gave everything to Him for the entire day, began enjoying your day, and the next thing you realize is—wham bam, by golly—you had a great day! Pain-free? Perhaps, perhaps not. But the pain mattered not, because your heart was in charge. Wow! That felt so good, you just may have to do it again.

Is that how we build faith?

One day at a time, my dear; one day at a time.

Sometimes even one moment at a time.

You've got it.

Let's talk more about the dreaded little mind.

Oh, such judgment! Try not to be so harsh. Your mind is a very useful tool, after all. Where would you be without it?

Of all the things I've lost, I miss my mind the most!

Cute! Very cute!

True! Very true!

I know you don't mean that.

You're right. I was just trying to be funny. Laughter is often the best medicine. I can be all stove-up in bed, practically in tears because of pain, when a friend will call me to see how I'm doing. Our conversation can begin in a dreary place, but then one of us will say something to cause us both to laugh. Before you know it, my pain is considerably lessened and my mood becomes uplifted and the world feels right once again.

A perfect example of the power of the mind. You began this letter feeling angry with God because He wouldn't (in your opinion) heal your back or ease your pain and suffering. We need to be very clear about pain and suffering, because they are two distinct perceptions: one does not necessarily go with the other. Pain is a physical sensation. Suffering is the way you may or may not choose at any given moment to respond to that pain. When people develop chronic pain, they often tend to get stuck in a "victim" mode.

Yes, I know what You mean. But it's hard not to be a victim! Sometimes I try so hard to change my life, to be in a better place mentally, emotionally, and spiritually; but it seems as though I get kicked in the teeth for my efforts. The harder I try, the more frustrated I become until I just want to give up or give in to the pain because I feel tired from the struggle. Pain, I. Ann, 0. Pain always wins.

I happen to know of many times that you won.

Name one!

I'll name two: Tuesday and Wednesday of this week.

Oh, yeah.

Oh, how quickly we forget! But that is exactly what your mind wants you to do: forget the good; dwell on the bad. When you allow your mind to be in charge, it will tell you over and over, like a stuck recording, how very miserable your life is and how horrible it is to have to live with chronic pain. Your mind will not show you the way out of this place simply because it does not have the answer. The way out of your misery and suffering is through your heart. I encourage you to allow God to show you the way to victory over pain—to be a victor, and not a victim.

But what about all of those books out there on the power of thought?

There is power in thought. Your mind is powerful. Dr. Norman Vincent Peale wrote a wonderful book on the power of positive thinking.

I liked that book. I felt empowered just reading it.

That is because it touched your heart. Jesus said, "As a man believeth in his heart, so is he."

Jesus was definitely a positive thinker!

Yes, indeed He was and is, but He understood that His power lay in His heart. Thoughts come and go. They can affect us positively to give us the kind of lives we truly desire or they can be our own worst enemy. You must guard your thoughts as though palace doors, protecting the king within.

I can see that. When I started this letter, I was out on my deck watching an absolutely gorgeous day come to a close, but the only thing I focused on was being upset because I couldn't go to a support meeting with my friend.

You were so caught up in negative thinking that you failed to see the beauty all around you. You couldn't allow yourself the absolute pleasure of the moment.

What a waste! Now I feel sad.

You're into punishing yourself, aren't you?

What do You mean by that?

I mean that you seem to enjoy dwelling on the negative. Yes, last evening was beautiful and you spent it being upset. So what? Today is a new day. This moment is brand new. Enjoy it!

I'm reminded of the verse in the Bible where Jesus said, "Let the dead bury the dead; come thou and follow me."

Jesus knew how to live in the moment. He knew that what happened yesterday was now dead and gone and matters not. The only important moment is now. Miracles can only happen in the "now," the present moment.

Yes, but what about our thoughts being creative and we create our lives today with our thoughts from yesterday?

Thoughts are creative. But if you want to live as your heart desires, I say to ask your heart, not your mind. Living in your heart today, this moment, will automatically, as though magically, create the life you want. Your desires will be realized, and your physical and emotional pain will diminish to the point of being nothing more than a fly on the wall. Wisdom lies in your heart. The most intelligent person in the world knows nothing if he knows not his heart. The wisest people in the world know their hearts extremely well.

Is that one of the benefits of meditation?

Absolutely.

I believe that spending time in prayer is important, but spending time in meditation is crucial; prayer is for your mind, and meditation is for your soul.

Very good, dear one!

Why, thank You! I know that it's only when I am quiet, still, and at peace that I truly experience my oneness with God. It is then that my soul is renewed and I know what God would have me do for the day or the week. Or perhaps, just for the moment. All I know for certain is that when I come out of meditation, I can face the world and my perspective on pain is back in its proper place. I feel wiser for having had the experience, and I feel better about myself for having the discipline to do it.

I used to pray for wisdom, knowledge, and understanding of Truth. I wanted to know things as Jesus knows them; somehow I intuitively understood that it didn't stop at the level of thought, that thought is only the beginning.

Everything, all of life as you see it, began with thought. It ends with wisdom. Where you are right now is somewhere in the middle. Wisdom is the result of your seeking to truly understand Truth.

I heard it explained once as being in math class trying to grasp algebra. Your teacher put the problems up on the chalkboard, and yes, you could see how she got her answers, but it didn't click with you until you worked several problems—or even many problems. Then one day the light bulb came on and you realized that you knew algebra.

Those seeking Truth have many so-called "light bulb moments."

Yes, I love those moments.

Can you look back at your life and see some of those moments?

Yes, I can.

Can you see how living with chronic pain has affected your life in a positive way?

It certainly has sent me on a different path than what I originally had in mind. I mean, I thought I was going to be in nursing until I died.

Your soul was dying in nursing.

Ouch! What do You mean? I loved nursing. My job was my life. How can You say I was dying?

Sometimes the truth hurts, until we understand it. Nursing is an honorable profession, and certainly we are grateful for caring and dedicated nurses, but you wanted more.

Yes, I can see that. I certainly wouldn't be here writing this book if I were still physically able to work as a nurse.

Your back injury gave you freedom. Oh, you fought the good fight to be able to continue working, but what has seemed at times a loss to you physically has been and continues to be a huge gain for you mentally, emotionally, and spiritually.

Boy howdy! When I don't let myself get bogged down by negative thoughts, I am grateful for my situation because it has been such a wonderful opportunity for spiritual growth. Every day I get to spend quiet time with God. I have so very much for which to be thankful: a husband who is absolutely the love of my life and who puts up with all of my nonsense;

two incredibly gifted, talented, and beautiful grown children; five grandsons who are equally gifted, talented, and beautiful; and two wonderful stepsons who always make me laugh even when I don't feel like it and whose love and support have meant the world to me. I had a dad who taught me by example the power of thought and how not to suffer in the midst of physical meltdown (dying), and a mom who also lives with chronic pain caused by arthritis and lupus and teaches me every day to never give up, that God will get me through, and that I can always find strength in Him.

You have a wonderful life.

I am so very blessed with an incredible family and wonderful, supportive friends.

See how much better you feel when you are thinking positively and coming from your heart?

Yes. I once read a sign that said, "If you want to get rich quick, count your blessings." I guess I can do the same thing for making myself feel better.

I like the sound of that.

So tell me more about living from my heart.

When you listen to your heart and let your mind take orders from your heart, instead of allowing it to go off on any old tangent it desires, the result is getting what you truly want in your life and not the things that you don't want. When the mind is taking its cue from the heart, positive thinking quickly becomes a very positive habit.

Like pain and suffering.

Yes. You may have pain in your life to influence and encourage your spiritual growth, but you do not have to suffer.

Because pain is a thing and suffering is our response to the pain.

That's right.   A perfect example is what you're doing right now.

You mean right this minute?

Yes.

What am I doing? I'm just writing.

Yes, but while you're writing you're having pain in your arm from holding the pen and paper in an awkward position.

I'm writing this while lying down in bed because my back hurts too much and I have severe spasms if I sit for very long. Then there are days like today when I cannot sit at all; I must lie down because of the spasms and the pain.

So you are in bed having bouts of severe spasms in your back and legs, and your arm hurts from writing in this position, yet you are not suffering.

Except that my arm feels like it's about to fall off.

Yet you continue to write.

Because I love this, and I don't want to stop.

Isn't it amazing how you can push your body to an extreme, yet you want to go on? You almost have to go on, because it "hurts so good."

That phenomenon has always amazed me. Athletes do it all the time. I guess this is where the mind comes in to do its thing, because the heart is engaged in doing what it loves.

That's it; you've got it! Everything is working together like a fine, well-oiled machine. Your body is going and going, your mind is pushing and pushing, and your heart loves it, loves it!

But sometimes I have to stop, or not even get started doing something, because I simply cannot make myself go.

That's perfectly okay. You know when to respect your body. An athlete wouldn't run with a broken ankle. He will know when it's safe to push and when it is time to rest.

That's the part I have the most difficulty with, the "when to rest" part, because it feels as though I'm resting all the time and I want to do so much more. That's when I get angry, like in the beginning of this discussion. I wanted to go to a support meeting, but I was having those severe spasms and had to stay in bed. I have innumerable times like that, and it quickly becomes frustrating, to say the least. My mind wants to go and my body says, "Think again." I can't find peace in that. This has been going on with me since my initial injury eighteen years ago, and, of course, has just gotten worse with the decline of my health. I'm angry—and I mean really angry— with myself for ever having back surgery; and here I am now, having had four. What am I supposed to do to heal these emotions?

Forgive.

Oh well, sure. That's just great. "Forgive" seems to be the one thing that I cannot do right now.

If not now, when? Every day you spend angry, either with yourself or the doctors, you are condemning yourself to hell for that day. Do you see that, dear one? You are making your situation so much worse because of your refusal to forgive.

But how am I supposed to do that? I've tried and tried. I've said, "I forgive you" a million times, but the anger keeps coming back to haunt me. You want to know the truth? I feel safer when I'm angry.

I'm sure you do, at least in your mind, because you've spent most of your life feeling angry. You have reasons to feel that anger; but it has not served you well, dear one. You've used it as a defense mechanism. I will tell you now that it has not defended you. Take a look back at your life (you don't have to look back very far) and tell me honestly how well the anger has defended you.

I certainly see what You're saying and have understood that for quite a while now; but it's what I know best, and I have a hard time living another way.

Actually, you have the most difficult time living the way you are now. It takes a great deal of energy to remain on alert and in the defensive mode all of the time. You can know that physically, because your body is in "fight or flight" mode and you have severe fibromyalgia flare ups. I ask you, where is the peace in that? There is powerful peace that comes with forgiveness. Perhaps if you had let go of your anger, you could have stopped to appreciate the ending of a beautiful day. Better yet, you began to write; now you are writing the book you've had a desire to write for quite some time. You expressed your feelings of anger through your writing, as you so often do.

Good point.

That's what I was talking about when I told you to see what healing looks like through the eyes of God. Perhaps you will always have back pain, but the healing you've received is the emotional healing you're receiving right now in this writing. Perhaps your back will be made whole again, but perhaps not. All things are possible with the omnipotent love of God. Yet everyone has their own paths to walk. The gift of peace lies in the midst of your pain, not the other way around. To live peacefully with chronic pain is an incredible beginning on the road to perfect health, if there is such a thing.

Many books have been written about achieving perfect health and healing chronic pain. But many arthritis sufferers, back pain patients, people with migraines, those who have fibromyalgia, and a variety of other chronic pain sufferers have a hard time with getting to a place of total freedom from pain. It's simply too big a jump to make from living day in and day out, every day of the month, or even the year, living with pain to ever imagine being completely healed.

That is why you and I are writing this book. You understand living with constant pain; you've done it for over seventeen years, since your initial back injury. You have great empathy for everyone else who has chronic pain.

Do I ever! It takes such a toll on your mind, body, and spirit. It wears you out and wears you down if you let it. The trick—or we could even say the miracle—is in not giving it that much power.

That is so true! That is the wisdom we want to share: to show others the way to freedom, the way to experience their own miracle. That will look different for everyone, but peace is our goal.

Don't let the turkeys (or the pain) get you down!

You have certainly strived for that from the very beginning of your experience with chronic pain.

Seventeen years is a long time. Four spinal surgeries with permanent (so they say!) nerve damage is a lot to go through, but I know many, many others have been through so much more.

You have experienced considerable suffering, and, as you said, many others have suffered greatly. You have given in to the pain at times, both physically and mentally, but you have never completely given up. Even your belief about the damage to your spinal cord and the scar tissue that your doctors said is permanent is unrelenting. You believe that your spinal cord can be perfect again, don't you?

Jesus told us that all things are possible with God, and He set about proving that throughout His life. I believe He's continuing to work miracles every day.

You're right.

But that's another book! Healing is just not for everyone, even me—not yet, anyway. I do believe that finding peace is a miracle all by itself.

Yes, and you have found that peace and want to share it with the world. Your strong desire to be peaceful in the midst of considerable physical (and emotional) pain has served you well. The numerous hours spent studying uplifting books, praying, meditating, and listening to lectures and workshops on tapes or compact discs have paid off for you. Now whenever you experience strong pain, you can control your thoughts and not get caught up in the otherwise agony of the ordeal. You control your breathing and can go into your inner sanctum, your heart, that peaceful place where pain is not allowed to go.

I love that place!

Spending time in meditation every day has become your healing time. The daily practice, the discipline is what has given you the ability to go there mentally, even in the midst of a severe pain episode.

Sometimes I do too much around the house or get delusions of grandeur and think that I can go on a major shopping trip, and my back lets me know in no uncertain terms that it is not happy. The result is severe pain. Sometimes even sitting up to watch TV in the den with my family is too much. I get reminded why I have been declared totally disabled.

You may be down, but you are certainly not out.

Hey, it isn't over until it's completely over! Until my body is dead and I'm gone, I intend to be productive—one way or another. My mom is a wonderful model for me. She's unbelievable sometimes; heck, most of the time! She goes and goes and goes even when she's in so much pain she can hardly stand it. She's seventy years old and runs circles around me. At times when she thinks she can hardly bear it anymore, she puts on her favorite gospel music or reads uplifting poems, and she gets recharged and ready to go some more. Her great-grandsons, my grandsons, always put a special sparkle in her eyes, too.

Everyone has their something special that recharges their heart and allows them to have the experience of peace, even with physical pain.

The trick is in allowing time for (or making time for) whatever works for you and to do that every day.

Yes. People tend to underestimate the value of quiet time spent in prayer and meditation, or listening to music, or taking a walk in the park—whatever gets them out of their minds and into their heart.

There have been plenty of times when I thought I was going to lose my mind! Many times the pain kept me awake all night for several nights and was relentless, not even responding to pain medication. Those are really difficult times.

Why don't you take this time to share with everyone what you do to get through those dark times?

First, I pray. Okay, sometimes that's the last thing I do, but I always end up wishing it had been the first thing I did!

What would you say is the best, the most effective thing you do?

I would have to say that the single most effective thing I do to get me out of my darkest times is to find a way to laugh. It's true: laughter is the best medicine. I'll call a friend, one of my friends who will not let me have what I call a "pity party," or I'll call one of my children. My son can always make me laugh, and my daughter will tell me a Daniel or Adam story (two of my grandsons, her youngest sons). If my husband or my two stepsons are around, they will make me laugh. If all of that fails for some reason, I'll put a funny movie in and laugh at that. The secret is simply to laugh.

Laughter opens your heart right away and serves as a great distraction.

Absolutely! Whenever my mom's pain gets to be too much, she gets on her computer and goes to her bookmarked sites of funny stories and poems. She says that she sits by herself at the computer and laughs and laughs—sometimes until she's literally in tears from laughing so hard—and before she knows it, her pain has subsided and she feels much better.

That is a great example of the power of your mind. Your mother could choose to stay in a place of suffering from so much pain, but she chooses to allow herself to laugh and thereby not suffer.

Yes. It is a definite mental choice we make as to whether or not we want to suffer and stay in a place of suffering, or allow ourselves to feel better simply by laughing.

It's a beautiful gift to give yourself.

Sometimes drugs help, though.

Yes, pain medication can be very helpful, but you will require much less of it if you add a good dose of laughter to your regimen.

It is our choice, isn't it?

Yes, it is. People sometimes don't realize the power of their mind or even their decisions.

It's easier to pop a pill or two.

Pill popping has become normal for many folks.

Do You think that will ever change?

It's changing right now!

Really? We're such a society of pill poppers. We can abuse our bodies in horrible ways; but hey, that's okay, because we have a pill for so many things that ail us! If medication is ineffective, surgeons can perform quadruple bypass heart surgery and make you as good as new (almost).

Medication is very helpful for many people.

Yes, and it also kills thousands of people every year.

But we are not writing this now to speak against doctors and medicine. We want to encourage people to do more for them and to help them understand how very powerful they are.

We are powerful, aren't we?

The mind is an amazing instrument that can be used to get you what you want or what you don't want. Peace or pain is a choice.

Many people don't think of it that way. They often feel like victims. I know I certainly have my times when I feel very much like a victim, as though I have no control over the pain or my situation at all.

You have come a long way, and you must give yourself credit for that. It's powerful to see and acknowledge the positive changes you make in your life.

I accept that.

Good girl!

I feel as though I have such a long way to go. I want to master my mind and use the power of my thoughts to achieve more peace and joy in my life.

Patience.

You've got to be kidding me! You expect me, the queen of "I want it and I want it now," to be patient?!

That's why it's called a virtue.

Yeah, well, some things are much easier said than done.

Like using the limitless power of your mind to feel better physically, mentally, and emotionally?

Like that!

Practice makes perfect.

Cute, very cute!

Funny, very funny! Isn't humor wonderful?

The character Archangel Michael (played by John Travolta in the movie *Michael*) said, "You've got to laugh; it's the way to true love!"

True love being God, Spirit, Life.

Yes.

Even your mind.

My brain is true love?

Not your brain; your mind.

My mind.

That part of you that is infinitely creative and more powerful than you can even imagine. Your mind.

The great unused!

To say the least.

Sometimes I wonder how far we can go.

As far as your imagination can take you. You are only limited by your thoughts.

If we have an original thought, it comes from God, right?

Absolutely.

So, HS, what is the best way to use our minds to live peacefully with chronic pain?

Begin with silence. One of the best ways to gain control of your thoughts is learning to quiet them. Jesus spent many hours preaching and healing and being with the crowds. But equally important to Him was His away time, because He had to rest and recharge just like everyone else. Most importantly, though, He wanted quiet time with God, communing with the Father, thinking on God's pure love.

Just imagine how we would feel if every day we spent twenty or thirty minutes in quiet solitude.

I can imagine. Can you?

I know what it does for me.

Go on.

It gives me a new lease on life. It smoothes out my ruffled nerves and helps to give me proper perspective on life and all the crazy things that occur.

What does it do for your pain?

It certainly helps me to keep an appropriate perspective!

It does even more.

Yes. I am off of almost all of my medication, and a great deal of credit goes to meditation.

The mind is extremely powerful in the area of pain management. With enough use it can allow anyone to get into a peaceful place and control their pain on their own, eventually allowing them to get off their medication completely.

Wow! That's a big jump!

Yes, but not an impossible one.

I know what you mean because I have experienced this for myself. I am happy to say that I am now off of all pain medication.

Good for you!

Why, thank You. While being totally free of medication is not a viable goal for many, if not most, people, it is important to me and is something that I intend to do for myself, for the rest of my life. I'm taking it one day at a time.

You must follow your heart and do what you feel guided to do and then act accordingly. When your thoughts, feelings, and actions are the same, when you say and do what your heart says, you will be completely free of conflict. You will be living harmoniously with God.

Where does the mind fit into this equation? What about the power of our minds, the power of thought?

I remind you that while your mind is indeed powerful, it is best if used in service of the heart. Your mind will misguide you and lead you to believe in false gods.

False gods?

While medical doctors and their tools—such as medication—are important in many situations, too much power has been erroneously given to them. Too much faith has been placed in what I call these false gods. Many medical doctors are like fire fighters. Instead of focusing upon health, being healthy, and being proactive in staying healthy, their focus is on disease and fighting a raging illness. This has led to many illnesses and disease that can be prevented, but no one cares because "there's a pill for that."

I want to be very clear about this. I understand what You're saying about parts of today's medical ways serving as false gods and I want to get into that further, but I'm not ready to go on yet. I want to get this down about the mind and the heart.

It is quite simple, really. Listen to your heart because it will tell you the truth and tell your mind to shut up and follow directions. Your mind has the power; your heart has the wisdom. All of those times in your life when you feel that you should do something, when you feel those little nudges or hear that little voice whispering in your ear—all of those come from your heart. When you meditate, you open yourself up to know, to feel, to receive guidance from Me, yours truly. I am all the things Jesus spoke of when He said, "My father will send for you a comforter." Well, here I am! How do you think you became able to have a conversation with Me?

Meditation and long walks in the park. Sometimes at church, especially in the music.

That's a great start. Just as God is everywhere, so am I. I am in a baby's smile, a beautiful flower that you "just happened to see." Who made your heart sing at the sight of the precious child's smile? Who made you quickly turn your head so you could see the flower?

You?

Me! I am always talking to you in so very many ways. Nudge, nudge, call your friend Jan, she's upset; nudge, nudge. You call your friend and just as sure as your heart beats, she needed to talk to you.

That was you?

It was Me! The more you pay attention to My nudges, whispers, flowers, feelings, the happier you will be as I will never lead you down a wrong path.

I hope You're right, because I would love to make this a book to share with others.

Didn't I guide you to write this, and didn't I tell you that it will be published and shared with many people?

Yes. You gave me a pretty large nudge.

I believe I have made my point pretty clear, but I do want to speak a bit more on this subject. I am with you always. I have never left you, nor will I ever leave you alone. When you ask me a question, I will answer. The answer may come in one particular way or a thousand different ways. Please pay attention, because the answer very well may be all around you—in the next phone call, a billboard you pass in the car, an ad or story in the newspaper.   It could be in the moon or the stars or the song on the radio.   Pay attention to your feelings. Have you ever had a gut feeling? That was Me!

It has taken me a long time to learn to pay attention, but I am always very grateful whenever I do because good things happen.

This book, for one.

This feels so good to me (writing this) that I could never consider it to be work.

Because you're following your heart.

Even my pain is diminishing. It has become less of an issue.

That is how you have peace with pain and end your suffering. Follow your heart.

Guard your thoughts.

That's right! Whenever you begin to get the "poor me's…"

Or have a pity party…

Tell your mind to be quiet…

Or just shut up!

Very simply, change your mind about the pain.

This sounds too simple!

The profound is in the simple. It's the ego, the conscious mind, that tries to make everything so difficult.

I have begun subscribing to the "less is more" theory.

Go on.

I have a friend who is an acupuncturist (and amazing healer!), and whenever I receive a treatment from her I am amazed with the effects of—as she puts it—a few pieces of stainless steel.

Simplicity!

I have another friend who is a Reiki master and who uses essential oils in her therapy sessions. I am always amazed with how wonderful I feel at the end of one of her sessions.

Profoundly simple is the way to God.

That's what I believe, but many if not most people have a problem with that.

Because they are so used to living in their minds, and the ego mind tends to make and keep things complicated.

If we see our lives getting complicated, we need to shut up our minds and open our hearts in ways that work for us.

That's right. You can laugh, sing, pray, meditate, watch a heart-warming movie, read an uplifting book, or call a friend. Whatever works!

That is the easiest way to stop our suffering and find peace?

Absolutely.

I get it! I am there! I think.

Practice. Remember, it's a choice.

It is a choice. I'm realizing that more and more every day.

Because you're practicing it. You are learning the wisdom of your heart and the power of your mind through practice.

It's a tool.

Which through use becomes a way of life.

Got it. Are we ready to move on?

You want to talk about your body.

Yes. Can we do that now?

It's your book!

THE BODY

The great used and abused!

Jesus said, "Know ye not thy body is a temple of the living god?"

Yeah, I've read that in the Bible, but obviously I don't have that yet. Just look at me!

People can be very abusive when it comes to their bodies.

The great unwashed!

On the inside.

What? Explain, please.

People are so very confused when it comes to how to treat their bodies.

Evidenced by how overweight and broken down we are.

I would say so.

But I'm so confused I don't know what to think! Low carb, high carb, no carb (carb being carbohydrate in case you have been off the planet for a while and missed the whole "carb" thing). Do we eat meat? What about dairy? And then there's that whole "sugar thing."

Well, we do not need to address these issues until you understand your relationship with your body.

Okay. I'm listening.

Do you realize the profound yet simplistic truth of your body being a temple of the living God?

No. I would have to say that's a big, fat no. I do fully realize that, as I am no master like Jesus.

Jesus showed you the Truth in many ways. As you would say in the language of today, He walked His talk.

One of the many reasons why I love and appreciate Him so much.

Rightfully so. When Jesus spoke of your body being a temple, He was speaking about it housing your soul.

Yes, I understand that.

Yet you abuse your temple so greatly. Do you remember the story of Jesus going into the temple and throwing a royal fit because of all the unrelated things that were going on there?

You mean like tax collectors and money changers and such?

That's what I mean. Jesus was upset because the temple was, in essence, being misused and abused. The temple was built for the work of God the Father and that alone. You wouldn't go into your church or synagogue today and expect to pay taxes or make business deals, would you?

Of course not! That sounds ridiculous.

It is ridiculous now and was two thousand years ago. Jesus knew the importance of keeping the temple holy, of respecting it and cherishing it, because it was a place to know and to be with God.

Our bodies are for that purpose, too?

Absolutely. Given that Jesus was so upset over actions that took place in that particular temple, how do you think He feels about your being equally abusive to your body temple now?

I never thought about that.

A temple is a temple is a temple. Jesus said your body is a temple; it houses the soul. So, My advice to you is quite simple: take good care of your body/temple.

Boy, I've messed this up. My poor body has been through hell and all because of the abuse I have subjected it to. Jesus must be in tears over this.

Jesus loves you unconditionally and does not get into guilt trips. If you want to feel guilty, hey, go right ahead. If you would rather begin right now, in this moment, to love your body, I am with you all the way. I will joyfully guide you down this path to peace. It is what God wants for you and intended for you. Nowhere in Jesus' teachings will you find that you were or are meant to suffer. If you are now suffering due to chronic pain, please stop it. There are definitive steps that you can take to set you free from the darkness of suffering and pain. We have spoken of several ways to use your mind to put you on the road to freedom and peace. Now I am teaching you the importance of caring for your body by first understanding that it is God's temple.

I guess people don't keep that foremost in their minds. I know I certainly do not.

What do you think would happen if you did keep that in your forethought?

I think I would eat much healthier, for one thing, because I'd feel guilty if I ate poorly.

Negative motivation, guilt. How's that working for you? Does it get you the results you desire, or do you just end up feeling even guiltier than before?

More guilty. But I'm so comfortable with guilt! It's so natural!

Guilt is anything but natural. It was created completely by the ego to keep you in your place. We could write an entire book about that, but let's stay on target here.

Are you saying that guilt doesn't belong in our world?

Definitely! It is a tool of manipulation used in the worst ways.

I can totally agree with that. But what do we use if not guilt?

Love.

Love?

You heard Me, and I did not stutter! Jesus went into the temple wanting people to act reverently and respectfully because of what it (the temple) represented. It was a place to commune with God just as is your body. Your body, in addition to housing your soul, is a means by which you may fully experience God. You get to see the beauty of a sunset. You get to feel and experience newly fallen snow. You get to smell and taste a freshly picked, fully ripened orange. You get to see and feel the unconditional love of a new life whether it be human or a kitten or a puppy. God created these things that are all around us to appreciate and love and feel joy. It is with your body that you experience God's love, so pure and so powerful. Your body is not meant to be abused and ignored. Life is a gift meant for joy and love.

Wow! I get that now. I have taken so much for granted.

You get so caught up in the thorns that you actually forget you are surrounded by roses.

Now we're back to perspective. Peace is yours for the choosing; it is a mental choice we make every moment of every day.

Yes, but there is so much more that you can do, additional choices you make—such as eating or not eating when you are already full, or deciding to exercise or not to exercise.

Thinking or coming to the realization that my body is a temple certainly conjures up a new perspective.

Let's discuss that perspective. I am not here to make you feel guilty in any way. God knows you do that enough to yourself. What I want is for you to come at your body from love. What would happen to your body if you showered it with love every day?

I can hardly imagine.

Well, please try. Newborn babies who are not held enough, touched enough, cuddled or hugged enough develop what is called in Western medicine a "failure to thrive." They begin to lose weight, will fail to have an appetite, and, without intervention, will die. What is the most important medical intervention for these babies?

Human touch. I helped care for a "failure to thrive" baby when I was in nursing school. All of us (nursing students) wanted to hold that baby.

Why was that?

Because it was such a sad situation. The baby was near death when it was first brought into the hospital. No one wants to see that. The only thing this poor little one needed was love. We were more than happy to provide that love!

Do you think adults need love?

Well, sure.

What would you say if I told you that much of the world's population is starving for love?

That makes me sad.

Do you feel motivated to do anything about it?

Like what? What can I do, and why are we talking about this in the middle of a little book about suffering with chronic pain?

Because you do not love yourself enough, nor do most people. Giving your body the love and attention it needs and deserves is a crucial factor in living peacefully with chronic pain. Before we can discuss nutrition, we must get you in the proper frame of mind to receive health and freedom from pain. You must realize that you deserve the best life has to offer and be open to receive all of that and more.

Wow! Silly me! I thought we were just going to discuss diet and exercise.

Oh, but there is so much more. We're not discussing symptoms here; we're getting down to the core of the problem, the reason you so readily accept suffering as part of life, as some sort of badge of honor.

I guess sometimes we do seem to love our pain a bit too much.

"A bit too much" is a gross understatement. Why, some have even built their lives around their diseases.

Isn't that going a bit too far?

Yes. Absolutely! You are going a bit too far!

Not me—you!

No, My dear one, not Me—you! It's not a "bit too far"; you are getting totally carried away.

I object!

Object away. The truth hurts sometimes, but only because you hate to fully see how completely overboard you have gone with these mind-created delusions.

Mind-created delusions? Come, come, now, be nice; I'm doing the best I can.

Yes, I understand that. But we are having this discussion so you can know better and thereby do better, right?

Yes, you're right. But I still don't see how all of this relates to my pain and suffering.

When you release your guilt, your fear, and your belief that you should be punished (for a wide variety of so-called "sins"), you can begin to love yourself. Your response to loving your body is the begin-

ning of finding peace. When you love yourself, your suffering will simply melt away.

I think that is happening with me.

Indeed it is, and it has been an answered prayer, has it not?

Absolutely. When I began letting go of my anger from being in so much pain all the time and started taking better care of myself physically, mentally, and spiritually, I began to get my old life back, only better. My family got the kinder, gentler, more loving wife, daughter, mother, and nana back. Even better than before!

You're beginning to understand what Jesus meant when he instructed everyone to "love thy neighbor as thyself."

It's that "as thyself" part that we get hung up on.

That's right. We can (and will) write an entire book about that in the future, but for now, please understand that the absolute last thing Jesus wants for you is to experience pain and suffering. He spent His entire life putting an end to people's pain, teaching them that they do not have to suffer for even one more minute.

Jesus loves us and wants us to be happy.

Absolutely. He fully understood that suffering comes from the ego mind and therefore is not at all necessary, ever. He suffered on the cross and then rose up from death to show you the truth about your body. He taught that heaven and earth shall pass away but God, Love, Spirit will live forever.

Are You saying that we won't die?

I am saying that your body will pass away, your sorrows, your pain and suffering will pass away, but your spirit lives forever. Once you allow Spirit to be in charge, your suffering will end and your pain will be just an annoying little inconvenience.

We will respect our bodies and treat our bodies well because they are the housing, the temples for our souls.

Exactly. You cannot serve two masters. Who are you going to pay attention to: God the Father or your mind? When you overeat, you are serving a false god.

Whoa! That's hard to hear!

The truth is hard to take for the mind, but the wisdom in your heart knows that it's true.

I do know that it is true; it's just difficult to eat healthy and exercise and do all the right things.

Because you have become a slave to food and a follower of the ego that tells you to go ahead and eat that big bowl of ice cream—it'll be okay. It's also okay to lay off exercising for a day, week, month, or year; take it easy for a while, says the ego. You listen because it is so very easy; you conspire to do the wrong thing. You are serving a master who does not have your best interests in mind. It actually runs its own agenda; it's the epitome of the devil himself, and he does not want you to live your best life and to constantly ask God what to do. He wants to be in charge as much as possible, and he will run you right into the ground. Pain and suffering are his allies.

He tries so very hard to convince you that God is the cause of your misery. I tell you now to serve only one Master and that is God, your Father. When you seek Love, you will find Love; when you seek peace, the peace of God will be yours and you will suffer no more.

Wow! That's deep! Can You explain that a bit more simply, because I'm not sure I got all of that?

God is not so concerned with what you eat as He is with how you live your life. Your egoist mind or the ego/mind part of you wants you to complicate your life as much as possible because it thrives on confusion and complexity. This means that you are not in alignment with God. You are not living in love and are therefore listening to him whom I call the "little mind." It's a bit like sitting outside on a gorgeous spring day with crystal clear skies above, the warmth of the sun on your face, and a pristine little creek babbling across the rocks. For a moment, all is right with your world, you feel peaceful, even hopeful of wonderful things to come. Then all of a sudden, here comes this bee. It's okay at first and you try to ignore it, but it becomes increasingly irritating until you find yourself completely annoyed. You go into the house thinking how wonderful your experience was until that stupid bee came along!

Let me guess: in this analogy, God is the peace and beauty and the bee is my mind.

You've got it! You could have ignored the bee and continued to enjoy the peace and harmony of the moment, but instead you chose to give the bee all of your attention and let it ruin your joy.

Why do I do this?

Because you're so caught up in the belief that you are not deserving of a wonderful, peaceful life. You want wonderful and peaceful, yet at the same time, this part of you believes that you have been bad in one way or another and therefore you are supposed suffer. It is a conflict that feels very real to you, and you're not sure of what to do about it.

What do we do about it?

Forgive yourself and love yourself. It's that simple.

Oh, sure! Easy for You to say!

Do you know how to recognize a truth of God?

How?

By its simplicity. God's messages of Truth are always simple.

Because we are the ones who try to complicate everything?

It's your little mind, the ego, the chatterbox that makes so many crazy rules. A perfect example of that is the diet industry.

Oh, man, you have hit on something there!

People are so confused they don't know what to believe anymore.

Will You put our minds to rest about nutrition and help us resolve our food issues?

No.

What? You won't even give us a hint?

I am not going to give in to your neurotic ideas about food.

That's it? That's all You're going to say?

I refuse to feed the monster.

I understand that we have gotten crazy with what we think, say, and do about food, but isn't that proof that we need Your help?

It is proof that you're paying way too much attention to your ego and not enough attention to your heart. When you begin to love yourself enough and understand that your body is truly a temple of the living God (your soul), any issue that you now have or ever had will simply fall away. Food will no longer be an issue, for loving yourself first will be your number one priority.

Loving myself first feels wrong. Everyone should come before me. That is what I was taught throughout my life.

I ask you this: How can you give away something that you do not have yourself?

I can't.

This is why you feel so tired.

Explain, please.

When you love yourself last, you are cheating everyone else. When you love yourself last, your family, your friends, the church, and everyone else gets cheated because the love you have to give away gets used up quickly and the well is soon dry. You have nothing else to give and you collapse in exhaustion, leaving almost everyone feeling dissatisfied and needing more. Jesus fully understood this when He said to love thy neighbor as thyself. He didn't say love everyone and then yourself. No, quite the opposite. You must come first, because you simply cannot give away what you do not have.

This is why it feels so good to give away what we want or need for ourselves.

Yes. That is the second part of Jesus' teaching—love thy neighbor. It becomes a beautiful circle of love. But you must understand the importance of loving yourself.

So when You were telling us to forgive ourselves and love ourselves, it is what we need to do for us first, so we are then capable of loving and forgiving others.

Forgive so that you, too, may be forgiven; and love so that you, too, may experience the full love of God.

This is how we end our suffering?

It's working for you, isn't it?

Beautifully. I am amazed with how my life is going these days. I'm not suffering, I have more energy, and my family is very happy because I am happy. Actually, "content" is more appropriate than "happy"; content and joyful.

Life is good.

Life is good.

You didn't get to this peaceful place by obsessing over food.

Quite the opposite. When I stopped being so concerned about every little thing that went into my mouth and ate until I was full, my world became a better place.

You quit feeding the monster.

What a monster it was! I had no idea how much I obsessed over food until I quit obsessing about it. What we are referring to as the monster is the mind. I would like to move to something that's on my mind right now and I believe is important to this discussion.

Living Peacefully with Chronic Pain

Go right ahead; you won't hurt My feelings!

I can't hurt Your feelings!

That's right! You should try it; it's an incredibly peaceful way to be.

I'll try to keep that in mind. But for now I'd like to talk with You about something. I have a question for You.

Fire away!

I would like to know how or what causes people to make positive changes in their lives. Some people will buy this book, but not read it for weeks or even months. Some people will read it, but will not follow our advice. Then there are others, I hope many others, who will read this and act upon what they have read. Is there one specific mental or emotional place where we get to that actually causes us to make important, loving, and positive changes?

Good question!

Why, thank You! What's the answer?

The answer, My dear friend, is quite simple: When you have suffered enough.

When we have suffered enough?

That's right. When you have suffered enough you will make specific, loving, and positive changes to end your suffering. Once you have absolutely, positively had enough, when you cannot take the pain a moment longer, you will act.

Do You mean when we feel hopeless?

No! Absolutely not! What I am talking about is very different from feeling hopeless. Quite the contrary. When you have had it with a certain situation in your life, when you have suffered enough to initiate positive changes, hope is what gets you moving. You have a sense of knowing that there is something you can do to find a more peaceful way of living.

That's why people buy lottery tickets.

You bet!

Oh, that's funny—"lottery tickets"…"you bet." Buying lottery tickets is betting, get it? We made a little joke!

Remember what I said about laughter?

It's good medicine?

That's right.   Laughter keeps your heart light. But, you were saying…

Yeah. People buy lottery tickets because they are hopeful.

Exactly. It is hope that eases the pain of suffering. When you have hope, you have everything. In the presence of hope, faith is born.   In the presence of faith, love becomes a possibility. In the presence of love, miracles happen!

So, it all begins with hope.

The end of your suffering absolutely begins with hope. When you have suffered enough, God will lead you to the right and perfect solution for you. It may be this book; it may be an acupuncturist, a massage therapist, a doctor, a minister, or even prayer. Be at peace knowing that at the precise moment that you say to God, "Enough!" the person or thing (like a prayer, scripture, or even a poem) will show up in your life.

That's exactly what happened with me! All of my doctors—my spine surgeon, neurosurgeon, and rehabilitation doctor—said that they could do no more for me. I was totally disabled and needed to accept my life as it was. Most of my time was spent in bed because sitting, standing, or walking was too painful. At the ripe old age of forty, my life was no longer working as a nurse and spending time with my family and attending church and volunteering at the Home of the Innocents (a refuge for abused children). No, no, now I was stuck in bed taking loads of medication all day and night.

You lived like that for a few months until one day you told God…

"I cannot believe that this is what You want for me! Enough already! Please show me the way."

Two days later you were introduced to the healing touch ways of Reiki (ray-key), and miracles happened.

It was amazing! While Reiki, which is simply a very gentle healing touch, is not for everyone, it certainly did the magic for me. Rather, God healed me using the hands of someone trained in the healing art called Reiki.

It was your answered prayer.

Boy, howdy! Was it ever!

While Reiki proved to be a very powerful healing tool for you, it wasn't the only thing you did.

No, that's right. I also read scriptures from Jesus and the Twenty-Third Psalm every day. I prayed and meditated every day, and I became a positive thinker by replacing every negative thought with a positive one. At least I tried to become a positive thinker. Some days I was able to do that more than others; but my heart was in the right place.

Years later, you had a fourth operation on your back for another ruptured disc.

I thought that one was going to put me under, but it didn't.

You have recovered from that by using the same means that you used after your third surgery, which was supposed to have rendered you completely disabled. From your experiences, you have learned how to end your suffering and make peace with your pain.

Thank God for my acupuncturist, for Reiki, for prayer, for Jesus (I'm especially grateful to Jesus), for my family and friends, and for increased wisdom, knowledge, and understanding of Truth.

Are you beginning to see the incredibly small role that food plays in putting an end to your suffering?

Yes, I think I'm getting it. We do tend to obsess over food and give it too much credit or blame for our joy or our sorrows.

Food is your friend. You cannot live without it. The mistake many people make is in giving it so much importance.

I love food!

Therein lays the problem. It would serve you best to merely like food and love God. Do not use food to fill the emptiness of your life. Let love fill in the empty spaces.

How am I supposed to do that?

Do you remember when you were stuck in bed because of your aching back, and you called the church secretary to ask for the names of people on the prayer list?

Yeah. When someone new called the church requesting prayer, she would call me and I immediately prayed for them.

It gave your life meaning and filled your heart with love. It also began your healing process, because what you do for others is also done unto you.

I get it! It's like what You were saying earlier: Whatever we need, we need to give away; in the giving, we receive in kind. So, if we need to be healed or even just want some peace, for our suffering to end, that is what we ask for in prayer, for ourselves and for others.

That's right. Peace can be yours because as Jesus said, "My peace I give unto you, my peace I leave with you." He was very clear in explaining that it was not like anything man could create; it was so much greater than that because the peace Jesus had in His heart was God's peace.

I have experienced some amazingly peaceful moments in my life, but I'm not sure if I have ever experienced the peace of God.

The full peace of God has only been experienced by a few people, but you can receive nuggets of it, as you have from time to time.

That's certainly good enough for me—for now, at least. Those moments that have absolutely taken my breath away are genuinely one of a kind. The whole reason for writing this book, though, was simply to help others end their suffering. When I was experiencing that awful, extremely depressing pain day in and day out, I wanted a break. I wouldn't even call it peace, necessarily. I wanted the darn pain to let up! I became suicidal because I thought that death was the only way I was going to get even the slightest relief.

This was when your pain was not managed or under control.

That's right. I thank God for my pain management doctor; but for months both before and after my fourth spinal surgery and flare-ups even to this day, medication is only minimally beneficial. Then I find myself deep in the throes of pain before I even know what has hit me. At that point, my suffering begins anew.

You have very specific steps you take to get yourself out of the suffering.

Yes. First and foremost, I remind myself that pain is physical and suffering is an emotional response to the pain. I may not necessarily be able to do much about the pain, but I certainly have a choice as to whether or not I suffer.

So you make that specific mental decision to be at peace.

That's right. I do that usually right after I cry and pitch a fit and ask God why in the hell do I have to have so much pain all the time!

Then I come in around that time and remind you that suffering is a choice.

Right! Then I pray. Then I get down to business. I may or may not take pain medication. I most certainly will schedule either an acupuncture or Reiki session as soon as possible, and then I'll distract my mind by watching a movie or something interesting on TV.

All of those things get you out of a suffering mode.

You got it! Now I have another question for You.

Okie dokie! Ask away.

The Holy Spirit just said, "Okie dokie," to me. No one's going to believe that!

Why not?

Because You're the Holy Spirit, the Big Guy, the Advocate, for crying out loud! Everybody knows You don't go around saying things like that!

Most people don't believe I say anything at all, so what do they know?

Ouch! Good point! Score one for the Big Guy!

I am being rather silly to remind you yet again to lighten up.

Got it. We do take life too seriously, don't we?

If you only knew!

I don't want to think about it! Although, thinking about being so serious reminds me of food, and I do want to talk about food even for a little while.

Really? You must discuss food?

Yes.

Okay.

Yea! Thank You so much! What advice, what sage wisdom, can You share with me about food?

You have to pay close attention, because this is important.

I'm all ears. What is it? Tell me, please tell me.

Don't eat so much!

Oh! What a wise guy!

Actually, I'm matching your personality!

I refuse to be responsible for Your attitude. Even though I can act like a real wise guy from time to time and believe that is one of my better qualities.

Hey, you know what they say, "If the shoe fits…"

…wear it. But you are the only true "wise guy" here.

Yeah, but we're just funning, and doesn't it feel good?

It sure does. Since I've begun having this particular conversation with you, I have naturally become much lighter. My mood has lifted, and my husband and two stepsons are very grateful. Even my dogs and cats seem happier. I talk more with my mother and my son and daughter who live in different parts of the country.

Your world becomes a better place simply because you open your heart to laughter. It's important to understand that laughing and letting joy into your life is a decision you make. Surrounding yourself with family, friends, even movies or books are powerful things for you. So many people who have chronic pain isolate themselves or become isolated because of their circumstances, and their isolation then becomes a large part of the problem. People are not meant to be alone all of the time, or even much of the time. People need other people, and if anyone tells you differently, they are not telling the truth. I say to you now, if you are suffering with chronic pain and feeling lonely or alone, you must reach out to others. It can save your life. Call a family member, call a friend, call your church, and call any church, just call. Ask someone to check on you every day, if not in person, at least by phone. You need it and you deserve it.

So many times, disabled people feel that they are a burden and hate to bother someone. I have certainly felt that way.

Get over it! That sounds mean, but I say it with great love. Please understand that the person who is helping you is getting as much if not more from their act of kindness, whatever it may be, than you are. That is the beauty of giving. You simply cannot perform an act of kindness without it being returned to you. The joy is more in the giving than the receiving. That is how God intended it to be, and that is how it is.

I love that about God! He's so cool!

The coolest!

Loneliness and isolation can be a serious problem for those of us with chronic pain.

It can lead to depression and causes the pain to feel even worse than it is.

Even in living with my husband and stepsons, two dogs, and two cats, I often purposely isolated myself by staying in my bedroom all the time, not even coming out to eat because my back hurt too much.

That leads to feelings of loneliness and depression caused by the fact that you have isolated yourself. This is when suffering begins.

I hear what you are saying and agree with it, but sometimes I want to be alone, especially if my pain is high.

That is fine for a few hours, or a day, perhaps even two days, but I must emphasize the importance of being out among others. As I said just a bit ago, but it bears repeating, you must reach out to others. Ask someone from your church to call you at least a couple of times a week. If you are physically able to get out and about, you must do so. Make a decision every day (and it is a conscious decision) to do something that is beneficial for yourself. If you have access to a computer, join an online prayer group or perhaps a Bible study group. Reach out to others who are in need. Join a support group for your particular chronic pain disease. *There are many activities you can do that take very little energy or effort, but can mean so much to you.*

I know of a woman who has chronic pain and often cannot attend church, but she's made it her mission to send cards every week to church members who have specific prayer requests. She writes personal, heartfelt notes to each person. She considers it to be her ministry, and the people of her church are always grateful to receive one of her cards.

What a wonderful story and perfect example of what I am saying. Jesus frequently, if not constantly, spoke of the importance of helping others. If you are suffering with chronic pain, there is no better way to end your suffering than to help someone else.

No matter how much pain I am in or how badly I think my life is sometimes, I can always pick up the newspaper, turn on the television, or call a friend to be reminded of how very good, how absolutely wonderful my life is, even in the midst of being in terrible pain myself.

Life is good.

Life is very good!

It pays to be grateful. Being grateful immediately gets you out of your mind and into your heart. Meaning that when you begin to thank God for all of the wonderful people, places, and things in your life, you cannot think about your pain; you cannot suffer. Gratitude opens your heart to the mighty power, peace, and love of God.

So being grateful is something else that we can do to end our suffering.

A powerful act it is, My dear one. Why don't you give it a try? You've experienced some pain today; let's see what it does for you.

Okay. I'll do it.

Most powerful and loving God, I thank You now for this beautiful, sunny day. Thank You for my husband as he is the love of my life and is so very, very good to me. Thank You for all of my family and the love that we share. Thank You, Father, for Christ Jesus whose love penetrates any and all pain. Thank You for a warm home, a comfortable bed, for my cats and dogs, because they bring me joy. Thank You for my friends; I am so blessed by their love and support.

I could go on and on!

Thank You, Father, for the love of Christ Jesus, for the knowledge that Jesus shares with me and with everyone who has ears to hear and eyes to see that the world is a wonderful place to be in, and that every moment of every day, I can choose to be bathed in God's all powerful love and to find peace right there in love.

Love is everywhere, and gratitude is an attitude of God.

Being grateful does ease my pain. It certainly ends my suffering.

You simply cannot be in both places at the same time. Suffering is a product of your mind. Gratitude comes from your heart, and when you become grateful, your mind is taking its lead from your heart. Your mind is no longer in charge; you are now living in your heart, and that, dear one, ends your suffering.

It nips it in the bud.

You've got it!

That's all well and good, but I can't constantly be grateful. I have other things to do, you know. Then before I realize it, I'm suffering again.

Practice makes perfect. Honestly. Give yourself time to make the desired changes in your life. If you have been deep in the throes of hell for many months or even years, allow yourself time. For some people, miracles happen very quickly; but for most people who live with chronic pain, the way to peace is a process. Every time you find yourself suffering, remember: I can choose peace instead of this because God's love is always, always with me.

I know! I understand what You're saying. When I initially wanted freedom from all the pain and suffering, I put index cards all over my house to remind me to think positively and that God loves me. God doesn't want me to suffer. The New Testament is full of Jesus' teachings to suffer not. One of my favorite quotes from Winston Churchill is up on one of my memo boards right now. He said, "If you're going through hell, keep going!" I love that.

Winston Churchill was a wise man and understood the impor-
tance of movement. Regardless of the situation, if you just keep going,
most likely you will get what you desire. Otherwise, you may get stuck.

I think that's what happens with so many people who suffer with chronic pain. We tend to quit moving—physically
and mentally/emotionally—and we get stuck. The less we
move, the deeper our rut becomes until one day we wake up to
discover that we are completely paralyzed. We ask ourselves,
"How in the heck did that happen?" Or, "How did I end up
like this—in so much pain and depressed? And for me, on top
of everything else, fat!"

It was a process. Getting yourself into that great big hole happened
over time. Getting yourself up and free from that place will take desire to
be free, determination to do what it takes, and love. Love yourself enough
to set yourself free, all the while knowing that God's love can conquer all.
You are never alone. Remember that please, for I am with you always.
My dear one, you were not meant to suffer. The physical, mental, or emo-
tional cause of your suffering matters not. Love can and will set you free.

I think I understand that. I have been in a rut—heck, a huge
hole—with my pain both physically and emotionally. Peace is
a process. It begins with a decision and a prayer. Enough!
God, I have suffered enough, and I truly want my life to change.
Please show me the way out of this mess, this hell, and let me
help others to do the same. How can I be of service?

Little by little, bit by bit, day by day, you have gotten stronger physi-
cally and emotionally and spiritually. You have decided to give meaning

to your experiences by helping others who live with chronic pain. In that, you have discovered the way to peace.

It may sound too simple, but peace truly is a decision. It comes from our heart, circles around us, and ends in our hearts. It touches us in every way—mentally/emotionally, physically, and spiritually.

Once you say that prayer of peace—"Enough, God! I wish to suffer not one moment longer; please show me the way to peace"—a team of angels goes to work answering your prayer. I, the Holy Spirit, will nudge you toward something to guide you, to let you know that your prayer is indeed answered. You may hear a certain uplifting song on the radio or on a television show, or read a magazine or newspaper article. You may hear a sermon that touches you in a specific way. A neighbor may be in need of kindness and prayer, and you are just the person to give that to her. You may hear a particularly sad news story that causes you to stop and pray for those affected and, at the same time, thank God for your good, realizing your situation could be worse. Thank God you're not those folks! Peace is a state of mind that can, with practice, become a way of life.

That's so very much easier said than done.

Yet it is a choice you make every moment of every day. Do you remember several years ago, shortly after your second spinal surgery, you were struggling with the pain as well as the emotional aspects of your situation and you met with your minister?

Yes, I remember. I don't think I will ever forget him or the advice he gave me, because it had a powerful impact on my life.

You were suffering. What did he tell you?

He told me to write, in my own handwriting, not on the computer, the Twenty-Third Psalm, and to read it (not recite it, but read it) ten times a day for ten days.

You did it.

I did.

It was life changing.

It was one of the most powerful things I have ever done in my life.

Why don't you write it here and now for everyone?

Okay. It will be my pleasure!

Psalm 23

The Lord is my shepherd, I shall not want. He makes me to lie down in green pastures He leads me beside still waters;

He restores my soul.

He leads me in right paths for his name sake. Even though I walk through the darkest valley, I fear no evil for you are with me,

Your rod and your staff—they comfort me. You prepare a table before me

In the presence of my enemies; you anoint my head with oil;

My cup overflows.

Surely goodness and mercy shall follow me all the days of my life, and I shall dwell in the house of the Lord

Forever and ever.

If ever you need lifting up, that is one scripture (among many) that can do it for you.

Amen to that! When I read that every day, ten times throughout the day for ten days, my entire outlook on life changed. Even with the first verse, God watches over me and provides my every need. That's how I hear that verse.

He makes me to lie down in green pastures, leads me beside still waters, and restores my soul—all these things are about being at peace. God reminds me that I am His child. I am loved, and being reminded of that instantly restores my soul.

He leads me in the right paths for His name sake. Is this what You meant, HS, about listening to our inner wisdom?

Indeed! Your soul is wise as it is one with God. Your heart has pure intent and cannot mislead you.

No matter what I encounter in this life's great journey, You are with me.

Have no fear, dear one, for I am with you always. I am your Comforter.

You answer my prayers, and blessings overflow. My cup runneth over! So many people fail to understand this verse, I think, for if my cup overfloweth, I have more than I need. I praise God for giving me so much that I may give to others as He gives to me. That's only the beginning, because goodness and mercy shall follow me my whole life long—for all the days of my life and I shall never, no, not ever, be without God ever again. I feel like yelling, Thank You, Jesus!

Amen! Glory to God! Don't you know the angels are singing now?

I feel like I'm at a revival, HS. Just me, You, God, Jesus, and the Hallelujah Choir!

How's your pain?

What pain? I am certainly not feeling any pain right now!

We filled you up with the all powerful love of God.

It is such an incredible feeling! It's peaceful, yet energizing. Serene. Powerful. Loving.

You can have this anytime you want it. Suffer no more. Be filled with God's love always.

We forget that love is everywhere; God is omnipresent and omnipotent. Let those who have eyes, see, and ears, hear. All you have to do is ask and God, I AM, is there, to ease your pain, to give you peace, and most certainly to end your suffering. I feel like we're at the end, that all that needs to be said has been said. To be honest, I thought there would be more.

Absolutely no more needs to be written about this. To end your suffering and to be at peace is all about asking for peace and thanking God at once for it. Peace is yours for the asking. Open your heart and feel the all powerful and ever peaceful love of God.

"As a man believeth in his heart, so is he."

—Jesus

"You are a child of God."

Thank You, Jesus!

Made in United States
North Haven, CT
08 May 2023

36365390R00046